Toward the Journey's End

Toward the Journey's End

D. E. YOUNG

Foreword by Mark J. Larson

RESOURCE *Publications* · Eugene, Oregon

TOWARD THE JOURNEY'S END

Resource Publications
An Imprint of Wipf and Stock Publishers
199 W. 8th Ave., Suite 3
Eugene, OR 97401

www.wipfandstock.com

PAPERBACK ISBN: 978-1-7252-5858-7
HARDCOVER ISBN: 978-1-7252-5859-4
EBOOK ISBN: 978-1-7252-5860-0

Manufactured in the U.S.A.   05/06/20

Contents

Contents

Contents

Contents

Foreword

DOROTHY YOUNG HAS PRODUCED a remarkable volume in *Toward the Journey's End*. It is a work that reflects the New Testament perspective that believers are "pilgrims" in this world (1 Peter 1:1) and recognize that "our citizenship is in heaven" (Philippians 3:20).

The book does a number of things, which includes offering a survey of salvation history by presenting central figures in the drama of redemption. Men and women who make at least one appearance are the following: Adam, Abraham, Isaac, Esau, Moses, Rahab, Achan, Hannah, Samuel, Jonathan, Hosea, Daniel, Ezra, Jesus Christ, Peter, Zacchaeus, the Rich Young Ruler, Judas, Barabbas, and Paul.

There is more though than the presentation of the flow of redemptive history. There is also what amounts to a survey of the major topics of theology. The poet touches on theology proper, anthropology, hamartiology, Christology, Pneumatology, soteriology, and eschatology.

Meditating on the pieces here presented, we find echoes of ideas presented by the dominant theologians in the history of the church. Young's emphasis on the Trinity reminds us of the Cappadocian theologians of the fourth century. The statement of Augustine—"You have made us for yourself, and our heart is restless until it rests in you"—resonates in these pages. The centrality of Christ and the cross in Luther reappears in these verses. Calvin's emphasis upon divine providence surfaces here yet again. The stress of Edwards upon the glory of God appearing in everything in nature carries through in this work.

In summary, this is a work of theology written by a master poet standing in the tradition of the Puritan divine William Ames who asserted in *The Marrow of Theology*, "Theology is that good life whereby we live to God." "Although it is within the compass of this life to live both happily and well, living well, is more excellent than living happily." Young helps us in this volume to learn how to live well on the journey to the Heavenly City.

I can do no better than to quote the words that Augustine heard from the mouth of a child so many years ago in a garden in Milan, "Pick up and read." You will not be disappointed, but rather changed and drawn closer to the Lord.

Mark J. Larson

Purity

Cleanse me in my secret heart
From my own defiling sin
Lest while glittering without
I be slithering within.

January 2017

On the Church Fasting and Praying for a Critically Ill Brother

O let our stomachs' rumbly cry
Be heard, our God, by You on high,
And let their empty, brief lament
Betoken help from Heaven sent.
Raise up the sick if You see fit
And be the world amazed at it.

January 2017

Dying Well

Grant me when I come to die
Sweetly in Your arms to lie
And though pain may be my part
Give me Heaven in my heart.
Let me gaze at the unseen
'Til the veil's no more between.
Give Yourself, the greatest Prize
E'en while Death shall dim my eyes.
Thus rejoicing shall I go,
Sorrow no more see or know.
Onward, then, unto the gates
Where the King of Glory waits.
He whom God has known shall be
Loved for all eternity.

January 2017

O Man, Greatly Beloved

O Daniel, stolen from your home
By hostile armies great.
O Daniel, forced in fragile youth
To serve a foreign state.
O Daniel, cast into the den
Because you, faithful, prayed.
O Daniel, sleeping with the cats
Because the angel stayed
Their ravenous ferocity,
Else you had by them died.
O Daniel, grieved at Zion's ills,
Confessing, fasting, cried.
O Daniel, how in Heaven's sight
Was your name magnified?
He showed you what was yet to come:
A preview did provide.
Not only loved by God on high,
The world's high Potentate,
But cherished and so greatly prized:
The blessing of your state.
Of dreams interpreter so wise,
By God beloved, distressed,
That kingdoms saw both fall and rise.
But still beloved and blessed.
If God should greatly love me then
Be still all murmured cries.
The greatest blessing man can have
Is to enjoy the Prize.

January 2017

The Census Tax

(Exodus 30:15)

> The poor shall not give less;
> The rich shall not give more.
> There is One Sacrifice
> That ever shall endure.
>
> One Father God, One Son
> That gave Himself for me.
> One Spirit active still
> To give me sanctity.
>
> All equal before God:
> No man may puff in pride.
> He chooses whom He will
> That shall with Him abide.

January 2017

Holy Perfume

(Exodus 30:37–38)

> The presence of the Lord
> Has such a fragrant scent
> No other drawing near
> No matter his intent
> Can make a sweet perfume
> More beautiful and fair
> Than that which fills the heart
> When Christ the Lord is there.

January 2017

Freedom

(Leviticus 14:1–7)

Two birds brought to the priest,
The one slain readily.
The other, dipped in blood,
Permitted to go free.

So He Who wore our frame
Was judged instead of me,
And sprinkled with His blood
I have my liberty.

Blest be His mighty Love
That brought Him to that place
To bear my punishment
And so assure me grace.

January 2017

Thanksgiving

Since, O my gracious God,
Your mercies are profound
Let songs of thankful praise
And gratitude abound.

January 2017

Artistry

To evolutionists
I will not give a nod.
Man, animals, and plants
Show artistry of God.

January 2017

The Mystery of Providence

I do not understand, my God,
Why You thus deal with me,
And yet I need not understand
But only bow the knee.

February 2017

Wedding Blessing

May you be so close together
From the first day to the last
That no matter what the weather
You may just one shadow cast.

February 2017

Barabbas

Blest be the Lamb of God
Who gave Himself for me:
The Son delivered up,
The murderer goes free.

February 2017

Criticism of Another Poet

William Blake, he was a flake.

February 2017

Atonement

(From Isaiah 6)

> O purge me with the burning coal
> That from Your altar came.
> O cleanse my secret heart within
> For love of Your own name.
>
> I would not find a sweet relief
> Were it not for the Lamb
> Your anger swallowed up for me,
> As wretched as I am.
>
> The only way You could forgive
> was to behold the blood
> My blessed Savior shed for me
> To make this sinner good.

> *February 2017*

Ocean

(From Genesis 1 and Job 38:8–11)
(After the Rev. Jim McCarthy)

> Behold the ocean, fearful soul,
> And how its billows ceaseless roll.
> It cannot pass the bound'ry sand
> For God restrains it with His hand.
>
> If He the mighty waters stays
> How can He not behold your ways
> And for your needs in grace provide
> If in His spear-pierced wound you hide?

Unto extremity I came
But He for love of His own name
Shall give me what is meet for me:
He promised. It must therefore be.

February 2017

Refuge II

(From Numbers 35)

O keep me in the city, Lord,
Where I for refuge hide
And let me not by pride or sin
Beguile my feet outside
Lest the avenger find my soul,
As guilty as before,
And on me vengeance well deserved
With wrath and anger pour
Until the death of the High Priest
Be reckoned unto me
For in His blood and offering
Alone I safety see.
Blest Priest, blest Sacrifice, blest blood,
The price of liberty,
Lord Jesus Christ, my only hope,
Who gave Himself for me.

March 2017

He Loves Me

He knows me, but He loves me still.
He knows each thought, both good and ill.
He sees my very heart's intent:
To Him all things are evident.
He knows the one I ought to be
But still in grace, my God loves me.

February 2017

Wilderness

It is not bread alone
By which each Christian lives
But rather God's own Word
Which to His own He gives.

With promises extreme
And hope that seems unreal
That man himself may see
And his dependence feel.

"For money keeps in touch
The kids" so says the wag,
But God will have us pray
And importunant nag

That He may show His power
In our extremity.
Therefore, I look for Him
To mercy show to me.

March 2017

Gospel

The cup of fiery rage
Was foaming fearfully:
God's wrath against my sins
Could not forgotten be
But Christ, Who loves my soul,
Came forth from peace of Heaven
To swallow down that wrath
That I might be forgiven.
He trembled at that cup,
So horrible to drink,
And bore Himself that wrath,
Too terrible to think.

Blest mercy, greatest grace,
And love beyond degree
From Christ, the Prince of Life,
Who gave Himself for me.

March 2017

Counting my Blessings

For what should I my Savior thank?
What has He given me?
Distress and sorrow, toil and pain
But also liberty,
Impoverishment and agony
And misery and woe,
But also His sweet presence that
Through all of this does go
Beside me and before me still
My heart to sanctify,
My will to bend unto His will
And my ways purify.

For anguish and perplexity
And guidance on the way.
For helplessness and hopelessness
And mercy day by day.
The man that walks can't comprehend
What God will do with him.
But trust Him in adversity
And all His mercies hymn.
All things together work His will
His children to chastise
And bring them safely home at last
So they enjoy the Prize.

March 2017

Pleasure and Dependence

Though pleasure sings a siren song
At once too loud and far too long
Yet trouble drives us to our knees:
"That does not hurt which does not please."
And help from Heaven does not descend
Until our cries for help ascend.

March 2017

Crumbs

(Mark 7:24–30)

If You but just the crumbs
Of Mercy give to me
It shall sufficient prove
And shall my plenty be.

March 2017

Strength

(Psalm 147:10–11)

Our God does not take pleasure
In men of strength and might
But he who fears before Him
Is precious in His sight.

March 2017

On the Death of T. B.

It was while list'ning to Your Word
That he the final summons heard
And closed his eyes but to behold
The holy city wrought of gold
And Christ the King to Whom he knelt
And Love's embrace eternal felt.

March 2017

Deaf Mute

(After the Rev. Jim McCarthy)

I could not hear or speak
Until You came to me
And took my soul aside
In Mercy rich and free.

Your fingers touched my ears,
Your hand my tongue beside
That I might hear You speak
And thus with You abide.

So Grace fit for my need
Your kindness gave to me
And thus my thankful songs
Shall echo endlessly.

Blest Grace at such a cost
You paid to set me free.
Bless, O my friends, the Christ
That bought our liberty!

March 2017

Contentment

Why should I be content
With what He gives to me
When I see other folks
That bask in luxury?

Because He gives Himself,
The best He can provide
And promises so sure
He will with me abide.

A cot becomes a couch,
A den a spacious place,
A tent a mansion is
Where Christ bestows His grace.

March 2017

Samuel: God Hears

She had no child nor hope of one
But in her soul's distress
She looked to Him alone to help,
Her barrenness to bless.
He heard her cry, He saw her tears
And in His mighty grace
He gave her what she asked of Him,
A son to fill her place
With little footfalls pattering,
With sweetest infant cries.
She offered unto God her King
The son that was her prize.
A mighty man that son became,
A prophet of the King,
For God remembered Hannah's prayer:
He made her sad heart sing.
So He regards the cries of His

Who long to see His grace
And shows them what is best for them,
Most notably, His Face.

March 2017

At the Bird Feeder

See now the little birds
That to my feeder flock.
They have no barns nor stores
Nor anything in stock.

So small, so weak, so frail,
Their worth not very great,
And yet He watches them
From His exalted state.

Their price may tiny be,
But not a one shall fall
Without His Providence
That oversees them all.

March 2017

On a Thunderstorm

(From Psalm 90:11)

Who knows Your anger's power
Which You in mercy free
Unleashed on Christ my Savior
Instead of crushing me?

April 2017

From Matthew 21:31,32

Who knows the pow'r of Mercy
Which our sad souls must know
For by it into Heaven
Shall whores and tax men go
Before the proud self-righteous
Who think that they are good
As if before the White Throne
In purity they stood.

April 2017

Earth Quakes

The earth could not behold
The death of Christ the King
But trembling shook with fear
To see that awful thing.

But when our Jesus rose
And burst the gates of Hell
It trembled then with joy
His victory to tell.

April 2017

And the Stone was Sealed

They sealed You in the tomb
As Daniel in the den
But could not keep You there
For You arose again.

The pow'r that shut the mouths
Of predators so strong
Was that that would not leave
You in Death's grip for long.

April 2017

Move Over, Monica

(Praying for the conversion of a man long prayed for by his mother)

Move over, Monica,
for by your side we kneel
And beg that God will show
the grace that sin can heal.
You prayed for fifty years
that your dear son might see
The glory of our Christ
displayed on Calvary.

And we beside you bow,
beseeching Him for grace
Requesting that He show
your son His blessed face.
Dear Lord, reach out the arm
of strength and let him live,
And for your mercy great,
we grateful thanks will give.

April 2017

He Humbled Himself

(Philippians 2:5–11)

It was from Heaven's highest throne
He stooped to make our hearts His own.
Himself He humbled, made a man
According to the Godhead's plan.

A servant's form our Jesus wore
And all our misery He bore.
His Father He obeyed always
E'en to the last of painful days

When He upon the cross our sin
Took up that He our hearts might win.
And for this work was raised to live
That to His own Himself might give.

All for the Father's glory spent,
Whose Justice could not just relent
But Anger hurled upon His Son,
The only Holy, Righteous One.

And then by God exalted high
Far higher than all majesty.
To Him shall all men bow the knee,
To Christ Who gave Himself for me.

Blest Lamb, the Spring of all our Joy,
Blest Christ, Whose praise our songs employ.
Blest Father, Kind beyond all thought.
Blest Spirit, Who redemption wrought.

April 2017

A Secret Servant

I am a secret servant:
a slave of Christ the King.
To worship and adore Him
and all my praises bring.

To serve His chosen people,
To cherish them as well.
To hold them up and help them,
All who escape from Hell.

To bear with all their weakness
As He has borne with mine,
To show His love in practice
Whose mercies are divine.

The greatest in His household
Shall be the lowest slave
Who cherishes his master
And those He came to save.

April 2017

Submission (II)

Come, my soul, bow the knee
Unto your God above
Who sends you pain and trials
As tokens of His love.

He knows the thing that's best,
Be it delight or pain,
And what will make your soul
Beside your God remain.

Therefore, submit yourself
Unto His gracious will
And trust Him for His grace,
For He will grant it still.

April 2017

Consider Him

(From Hebrews 12)

Think, O my soul, on Him
Whom sinners did oppose
Lest you discouraged be
And faint before your foes.

As yet unto your blood
You have not sin defied,
And you forget that God
His sons alone will chide.

Make strong the feeble knees.
Let feet not turn aside
But trust Him for His grace
Who will with you abide.

April 2017

Esau

(From Hebrews 12)

O Esau, for what did you sell
Your birthright on that day?
Profane, you chose a trinket small,
Your blessing cast away.

You sought the blessing once again
But it was far too late.
Your tears that fell could not undo
Your sin, for it was great.

April 2017

Paul in Peril

(From Romans 8 and II Corinthians 11)

In peril from false brethren,
In danger on the sea,
In beatings and imprisonment
As God's will proved to be.

Shipwrecked and stoned and beat with rods,
So many stripes received,
By countrymen was mocked and scorned
Because he truth believed.

In fastings and in watchings oft,
In hunger and in thirst,
But serving not his comforts all
But Christ, his Master, first.

So then, my soul, can you compare
With him in your distress?
And yet this saint, from dungeons dark
His voice raised, God to bless.

For all things work together still,
The bright things and the dark,
To keep the suff'ring saint alive
Within salvation's ark.

So, my soul, trust the God that smites
And rest within His arms.
Who cannot fail and cannot lie
Will keep your soul from harms.

April 2017

The Tenth Commandment

O Achan, did you dare
To covet earthly things
Defying God the Lord,
The mighty King of kings?

And Judas, for what cause
Did you our Christ betray?
Did greed so capture you
You could not get away?

How dangerous the sin
We pass so lightly by.
To covet before God
Is to deserve to die.

April 2017

These Things Were Our Examples

(From I Corinthians 10)

They all escaped from Egypt,
They crossed the Red Sea all.
The waters on both sides of them
Were a protecting wall.

All baptized into Moses
In sea and in the cloud.
All heard the roaring thunder
At Sinai, dark and loud.

But they forgot their Savior,
Their great Redeemer King.
They bowed themselves to idols,
Profanely trespassing.

They fell to fornication,
Their Lord provoked to ire,
And tempting Christ, they suffered
The serpents' venom fire.

They murmured, discontented,
Provoked Him to His face.
They scorned His faithful servant
And then despised His grace.

All this was for our profit
That we should learn to fear
And not provoke our Savior
But hold His mercy dear.

Let him who thinks he's standing
Take heed lest he should fall.
Let us heed His commandments
And keep His statutes all.

For nothing can befall us
That we cannot endure
Because our God delivers
And gives us rescue sure.

Blest Grace that is sufficient
For all our pilgrim way.
By Grace alone we'll conquer
Until the Final Day.

April 2017

Personalized Grace

(From Mark 8:22–26)
(After the Rev. Jim McCarthy)

You took my hand and led me out
Far from the busy square.
You spat into my blinded eyes
So I knew You were there.

You healed me gently, step by step,
My weak faith strengthening.
You gave me back my sight again,
My blindness banishing.

Blest Grace that stooped so very low
To heal my blinded soul
And show instead the Glory of
The Christ Who made me whole.

April 2017

Facing an "Adverse" Providence

My soul, if you cannot submit
To Providence as God sends it
Then tell me what you mean to do
When God bids Death to come for you.

May 2017

Watered With Tears

May it please Thee, gracious King,
that the tears which I have shed
over things both sharp and hard
which have bowed my weary head
moist instead the precious seed
that they may not wasted be,
growing wheat instead of weed,
bringing glory unto Thee.

May 2017

On a Root Canal

My dentist sometimes hurts me
Although he is not mean.
But teeth diseased must be removed,
The rest kept nice and clean.

And so it is when God afflicts,
Though it may hurt a lot:
He does this for our benefit
To cleanse from every spot.

Therefore, be still, my sorry soul,
And see you bow the knee.
Though other friends may love you well,
None loves you more than He.

May 2017

Fig Leaves

My God, I am ashamed
Of what I am and who,
My sins before Your face,
The evil things I do,
The things I fail to do
That ought by me be done,
The secret faults and known,
Need cleansing, every one.

I cannot hide myself
Or cover up my shame
I beg You to forgive
For love of Your own Name
And for His sake that died
That I might ransomed be
Therefore, I pray, my God,
Be merciful to me.

May 2017

Victory

The strong may not prevail,
The swift not win the prize,
But he who hopes in God
Shall see with his own eyes
The vic'try won at last
At least when life is done,
Though he see nothing else
Shall gaze upon the Son.

April 2017

On the Mortification of Sin

May this splintered, rugged cross
Be the death of sin to me,
Making baubles of this age
Burst and pass me harmlessly.

Let me then obey the Father
When He bids me sin to kill,
Choosing rather to bear sorrow
Than resist His Holy Will.

Let my death to unjust pleasure
Be to me but life anew
Finding all my precious treasure,
Blessed Jesus Christ, in You.

May 2017

Give me Jesus

Give me Jesus Christ, most blessed,
Passing beautiful and fair,
Give me, Lord, this gracious Savior,
Of all precious ones, most rare.

I am weak and full of darkness
But I long to dwell with Him
In the glory of His beauty
Free from sorrow, dark and grim.

Give me Him, my priceless treasure,
And I will all else forego.
Give me Him, my great Redeemer,
And I shall not sorrow know.

Best of all, the mighty Sovereign,
Over all things glorified.
Give me Jesus with contentment
And I shall be satisfied.

May 2017

The Smell of Sanctifying Providences

(After Charles Spurgeon)

Sometimes, a work may tell us
The clock chimed midnight's bells
But far more often, really,
Of prison damp it smells.

May 2017

Gethsemane

(After the Rev. Dr. Stephen Jennings)

How dare you, soul, pass lightly by
The death He was about to die
At which your Lord was sore amazed
While you at God's wrath stand unfazed.
With bitter tears and anguished cry
He prayed the cup would pass Him by,
But seeing that was not God's will
He chose the cov'nant to fulfill
And poured His soul out unto death,
Obedient to His final breath.
He heard Him for His piety,
Who bore my sins entirely.
For this, by God exalted high
That all men might Him magnify
And bless the grace and mercy free
Which Jesus Christ bestowed on me.

June 2017

Petition

I beg You, Lord, to spare the life
Of this small child, as yet unborn,
For grief has such a bitter taste
Her mother would be so forlorn.
Have pity, for I cry to You:
Jacob is small, nor can he stand
Nor bear the grief about to come
Unless upheld by mighty Hand.

June 2017

Emptiness

Lord, I am empty: fill my soul with Thee.
Let me the beauty of Thy glory see.
Let me the music of Thy name declare
As in the suff'rings of the Christ I share.

June 2017

Life

Since Thou of Life the fountain art
And all things live because of Thee
Since Thou hast overcome our death
Be Thou the death of sin to me;
What stronger foe have we than death,
But in Thy mighty Majesty
Since Thou hast overcome our death
Then overcome the sin in me.

June 2017

Confrontation of the Fall

Where are you, Adam? Why so hide?
For nakedness you did not know
But now you know it bitterly,
The sin and shame your acts bestow.

Why cast the blame upon your bride
And on your God, the Holy One?
The guilt is yours, and mine as well
For by your sin I am undone.

But God in mercy rich and free
Did not you drag from out the trees
But merciful provides for you
And from your sin and death He frees.

The Second Adam took my place
Who stood before the judgment seat
For all my sins condemned to die
Who bore God's wrath's eternal heat.

June 2017

Communion Meditation

(Hebrews 10:13)

Our Altar, where the Prince of Life,
Our peace off'ring, was slain
Affords a richer, sweeter feast
Than money can obtain.

June 2017

Thy Will Be Done (II)

(Luke 6:46)

> If with my lips I call You Lord
> Then be Your law in heart adored.
> And let me choose what You command
> As in Your presence sweet I stand.

June 2017

Purity (II)

(Proverbs 22:11)

> Let me, my God, love purity
> of heart, and be it found in me.
> And may it so my sin displace
> That e'en my words be filled with grace
> That Heaven's King my friend may be
> If purity be found in me.

June 2017

The Danger of Hard Thoughts

> What caused our first iniquity?
> What brought the chastening rod?
> Was it not when our mom indulged
> Hard thoughts about our God?
> So let me keep a careful watch
> On what my mind might say,
> Lest from His mercy and His Grace
> My heart should seem to stray.

June 2017

Cleaving to Christ

Unto my Savior let me cleave,
For Him my sins to hate and leave,
To hear His voice and love His ways
Until the last of earthly days.
Temptation's waves around me roll
Endangering my very soul.
I'm sinking, Lord, I pray to Thee
My Life Preserver sure to be.

June 2017

Loving Christ

(Matthew 10:36–38)

If I love something more than You
I show myself unfit
To follow in Your footsteps, Lord,
To earthly trinkets knit.

I must love You more than myself,
More than my friends and family.
If You are not first in my heart
I cannot Your disciple be.

So let me take my splint'ry cross
And bear it even unto death
For You I love, O blessed Christ,
And will love to my final breath.

June 2017

Hosea (II)

(After the Rev. Jim McCarthy)

> He stood down at the aisle's end,
> My gracious Lover and my Friend.
> I came in through the open door,
> A wretch defiled and a whore.
> I dared not raise my eyes to see
> The Savior Who had summoned me.
> I heard His voice; He bade me come
> And offered me His heart and home.
> Amazed, bewildered did I stand
> To look upon His pierced hand.
> With every step I took towards Him
> My rags grew whiter that were dim
> And then became a glorious dress,
> The garment of His righteousness.
> I left behind my former life
> To be His treasure and His wife.
> Blest Love that paid the price of sin
> That I might freely enter in
> And see the Beauty and the Grace
> That shine in my Beloved's face.
> One thing, my Jesus, would I know:
> How could You ever love me so?

July 2017

Fidelity

From Ezekiel 16

> My father was an Amorite:
> A Hittite was my mother.
> They did not love me, nor was I
> Beloved of any other.

You passed by and You saw me there
In filth and my blood lying.
You could have passed on by me
For You saw that I was dying.

And yet in mercy wonderful
You washed and swaddled me.
Though I was vile, You bade me live,
In grace so rich and free.

I lived and grew and came of age,
And then You married me
And swore to me Your covenant,
That You would faithful be.

You made me beautiful and fair,
With jewels covered me.
My clothing was embroidered, and
I dined on plenty free.

So also with Your own of old:
On them Your Grace You spent,
But not responding to Your love
To other loves they went.

Unless You, Lord, should make me chaste
I too will run away
And seek for happiness and joy
In trifles of the day.

Since I cannot keep Covenant,
I pray You show Your strength:
Keep covenant instead of me
And bring me home at length.

Perverse I am, and all unclean,
In every way defiled.
But pity me and keep me close
As Your beloved child.

July 2017

Discontentment

Beware, my soul, what your heart says
To God's supreme decree
And let you wisely shut your mouth
And to Him bow the knee.

July 2017

The Rich Young Ruler

(After the Rev. Jim McCarthy)

He ran to You and bowed the knee,
inquiring after life.
You brought the Law to bear on him
just like a surgeon's knife.

He thought that he was pretty good
for outward laws he kept
forgetting that You see the heart
and coveting is theft.

He went away sad and dismayed
because he would not give
for life the price of all his things;
therefore he could not live.

You let him have his heart's desire,
the things of this world's stuff.
He chose to die, believing You
Yourself were not enough.

So, my soul, what do you desire
or what price will you pay
to have the very Son of God
as your own on that day?

What will you say when God demands
a just account and true?
Though you are guilty, yet the Christ
shall stand and plead for you.

July 2017

Law and Love

If I love myself supremely
then how quickly would I dare
to reach out for fruit forbidden
though He bade me to forbear.

If I love my gracious Savior
then the Law that He commands
will be cherished in my heart and
also practiced with my hands.

So then give me, gracious Savior,
greater, growing love for You
so that I before my Sovereign
may increasingly be true.

July 2017

Meditation on Having my Money Stolen

(After reading Psalm 18)

Be angry, O my gracious God,
At those who me oppress.
Regard their actions and their words
Who caused my soul distress.

Hold not Your peace, my Savior dear,
Hide not Your face from me
But see the wickedness of men
Who with my goods made free.

Ride on a cherub and draw near,
Come in a mighty storm
Of anger and of vengeance pure
And cause them great alarm.

I could not overcome them, Lord,
They were too strong for me
But in Your perfect justice, please,
O may You angry be.

Remember me and do me good
And for my needs provide
For in Your mercy and Your grace
From wickedness I hide.

July 2017

From Isaiah 54

Sing, woman that has borne no child.
Sing, barren widow and defiled,
For children have you more than she
That happily might married be.

Enlarge your tent. Your cords stretch out
For o'er the Gentiles shall you shout.
Your seed shall rule o'er enemies,
And hostile cities shall they seize.

Be not afraid nor be ashamed:
No more with ridicule be named.
Reproach lay by nor pain recall
For you shall triumph over all.

Your God has called you from distress
And with Himself He will you bless.
Though grieved and sorrowful you be
Yet shall you mighty blessing see.

A little while He turned away
But now will comfort you this day.
In wrath He hid from you His face
But now you shall enjoy His grace.

For as the earth no more shall flood
So He will do you naught but good.
No more shall your God angry be,
And you His wrath shall never see.

The mountains may be chased away,
The hills flee in that dreadful day,
But Covenant He cannot break
If He should promise undertake.

Afflicted one, you shall be fair,
A city pure and without care.
Your walls shall be of precious stone,
And you shall never be alone.

Your children shall in safety dwell
And with your seed it shall be well.
And never more shall you know fear
For God, your Savior, shall be near.

July 2017

The Gilded Anchor (II)

(after the Rev. Jim McCarthy)

How hardly shall the rich
To Heaven enter in!
For riches numb the soul
To feel not its sin.

How blessed are the poor
Not for their lack of things
But for their faith and hope,
Gifts of the King of kings.

A life cannot be measured
By things one may possess
But rather by the love
Which humble hearts shall bless.

July 2017

On the Cross

It was because we broke the Law
Of Love to God and Love to man
Our Savior hung upon a cross
Beneath the heavens' darkened span.

The horizontal piece may be
The lesser law we broke but yet
The vertical that points to God
In fact connotes the greater debt.

Ten words: two parts: two Laws for us
That form for us our crosses too
For we must choose against our wills
Unto our Sovereign to be true.

August 2017

From Psalm 143

O hear my cry, my God:
To my request give ear.
In faithfulness reply:
In righteousness O hear.
And sit not down to judge
For I am far from clean.
In Your sight man is vile
And every man is mean.
The enemy oppressed
And smote me to the ground.
And I in darkness dwell
As those whose graves are found.
My heart is overwhelmed:
My spirit desolate.
The days past I recall,
On Your works meditate.
My hands stretch out to You,
My soul athirst must be:
O hear me lest I die
And perish utterly.
Make me to hear the sound
Of lovingkindness free:
The rescue drawing near
To save the poor like me.
Teach me, Lord, to obey:
In Your ways walk in peace:
O raise me up to life
And grant my soul release.
Look on mine enemies:
Forgive or judge them still
For I Your servant am:
Teach me to do Your will.

August 2017

On Seeing a Rainbow Very Faintly

Sometimes, when tears becloud mine eyes
I cannot see across the skies
The promise shining bright and pure
For pain besets me more and more,
But yet the rainbow still remains
Despite the presence of my pains.
God knows what He has planned to do,
And to Himself He must be true.
Therefore, be still, complaining heart
And wait for Him to show His art.

August 2017

Beatitudes

How happy is the humble heart
That sees his faults and sin
And thinks upon his poverty
For Heaven shall he win.

And bless'd is he that, mourning, weeps
Because of wretchedness
For comfort shall come forth for him
And perfect blessedness.

And happy is the humble soul
That walks in gentleness
For patiently he bears with all
And earth he shall possess.

Bless'd are the hungry, thirsty souls
That long to righteous be
For they by grace shall see their wants
Fulfilled in mercy free.

And happy is the merciful
In his extremity
For mercy sure shall find him out
And then his portion be.

Bless'd are the holy, pure in heart
That long to righteous be
For they with joy shall Him behold
When they His face shall see.

And happy those that make the peace
Though facing conflict strong
For folks shall call them sons of God
And He shall be their song.

And bless'd are you when men revile
And vilify your name:
All kinds of sins they charge you with
But falsely in their shame.

If sadness now should be your part
Rejoice, my soul, and sing:
In Heav'n you have a holy prize:
The favor of your King.

August 2017

Flood and Fire

When judgment's thunders echo round
Let me in Christ the Ark be found.
When rains the fire from the sky
Let me to Jesus nestle nigh.
E'er anger surges round the Ark
And wrath this bright world renders dark
Let me unto the Refuge run,
To Christ alone, the mighty Son.
To righteousness will I lay claim

But only that found in His name.
Though this world burn with final fire
To new made earth will I aspire.
To Christ alone for grace I flee,
A Refuge strong enough for me.

August 2017

Triumphal Entry

Not on a stallion strong
Nor on an iv'ry throne
Came Christ the King of kings
To walk among His own.

To children's shouted praise
Upon a donkey's foal
He came to bleed and die
To make His people whole.

If children did not cry,
His praises did not shout,
The rocks would have His praise
With stony voice cried out.

Not for an earthly realm
Or empire strong and great
But an eternal crown
Which after death did wait

A Savior strong enough
To rescue even me;
From sin and death and Hell
His people to make free.

Their voices rang again
In one week's little space
Then crying for His blood
Which He poured out in grace.

But when He comes again,
A white war horse astride,
He'll crush His enemies
And take us to His side.

Then shall old Death be dead
And pain and sin be gone
And all the world cry out
The honors of the Son.

August 2017

Trial

(From James 1)

The trial is so strong,
So sharp it seems to be
But grace by it is grown
And patience you shall see.

Let patience do her work
And bring you down to dust,
For he who waits for God
In Him may safely trust.

August 2017

The Honey Trap

Temptation pleasure sometimes vends,
Sometimes a sad refrain,
But pleasure is more dangerous
To man than bitter pain.

August 2017

For O.D.

How did the Serpent Eve deceive, though man rebelled with open eye,
Instead of being more like God Himself, the man began to die.

And so Death passed down to all men for all in Adam Law defied
So even babes and children fair by Death were murdered, and they died.

But life is found in God the Son, the Second Adam glorified,
And those for whom He gave His life in peace forever shall abide.

Nor can old Death their lives destroy, for safe they dwell in Heaven fair
Nor can the second Death them slay when once His own are settled there.

September 2017

Hurricane Irma

Here come the clouds, the winds, the rain,
And by them some already slain,
But darker still shall be the Day
When Heaven and earth shall pass away.

What power does Heaven's anger hold
For those who Him for greed have sold?
Lord, give me love of Christ alone
And let me kneel before His throne.

Let me love Jesus more than all
And at His feet forever fall.
Blest Savior from the wrath to come
And for my soul, eternal home.

September 2017

Thanksgiving (II)

Long have I prayed without relief:
Long struggled on in pain and grief,
But God that reigns alone on high
Is not a man that He should lie.

Because He promised to provide
My needs and wants have been supplied.
Blest Grace by which He comforts me,
A pledge that I His face shall see.

"Praise God, from Whom all blessings flow!
Praise Him, all creatures here below!
Praise Him above, ye heavenly host!
Praise Father, Son, and Holy Ghost!"

September 2017

Provision

Not for my righteousness
Nor knowledge nor yet skill
Have You Your grace bestowed
According to Your will.

No, it is all of grace
That You Your blessings give
That by Your kindness great
Before You I may live.

Through wilderness I went,
A dark and bitter way,
Awaiting promised grace
And promised vict'ry day.

Now in the land of life
I see the mercy shown
You promised to bestow
Upon Your very own.

Blest Father, merciful
E'en when Your sons You smite
For chastisement gives way
To everlasting light.

September 2017

Anastasia

Though I lie down when Death takes me
Yet in God's mercy rich and free,
But once alone I cross that stream
For He my person did redeem.

The second death cannot me smite
For Jesus is my heav'nly light.
When I shall see His visage shine
Forever more shall He be mine.

October 2017

Three Trees

Forbidden fruit we did partake
And enmity thereby did make.
He said that we would surely die
And thus it is as time goes by
But on another cursed tree
He hung Who came to rescue me
And by His life and death alone
I have hope I shall be His own
And taste at last the tree of life
Part of His bride, the Savior's wife.

October 2017

For Robert Samuel Dyer (III)

Sweet tiny child, by mercy given
And by death taken back to Heaven
One year ago. Dear, I would hear
How, in His presence, was your year?

We grieved for you, but you had joy
Peace, happiness, without alloy.
Dear child, we still await the day
When we shall see you laugh and play.

October 2017

The Greatest Commandments

Gracious Lord, Your yoke is easy:
You command us from above
More than any other statute
That to You we give our love.

And that we should love our neighbors,
Do them good instead of ill.
To obey is sweet and precious
When, renewed, we love Your will.

O that every day more closely
We might walk within Your law
That we might show our thanksgiving
For Your grace to You, our Awe.

October 2017

And Abram Went Out

At God's command, Abram went out
Unto a land as yet unknown,
But Him he knew, the one true God,
The God Who was his very own.

Not knowing where you're going to
Has benefits perhaps untold
For Sarai could not make you stop
So that directions might unfold.

October 2017

Submission (II)

I do not understand Your ways
But since You gave Your Son to die
That I might have a pardon sealed
To You alone I bow the knee
And do not rudely ask You why.

October 2017

Understanding

It is not in man that walketh
His own ways to understand
For God's Providence is mighty,
And He rules us by His hand.

Therefore, let us then be busy
All His precepts to obey:
We shall see His purpose ripen
To fruition in that Day.

October 2017

Thoughts on Psalm 8

(After Mr. Stephen Spinnenweber)

Creation does not whisper
God's glory from the skies.
It shouts aloud His greatness
And His name magnifies.
And children's lips pronouncing
His praises, being weak,
Upon His glory focus,
The humble and the meek.
For after making Heaven
And moon and stars so fair,
He made man in His image:
None other can compare.
As if His left hand using
He overthrows His foes
His strength shines out through weakness,
His mighty glory shows.
And Christ, the glorious Victor,
The ruling, reigning King,
Has all things put beneath Him,
All creatures worshipping.
So we look for the vic'try,
When He makes all things new,
Almighty Lord, we worship
And bow the knee to You.

November 2017

He Knows

When solitude its sadness breathes,
When vague confusion my way weaves,
When grief or sadness overflows,
Be still, my soul, He knows, He knows.

When disappointment clouds my eyes,
When trouble overcasts my skies,
When my own way I can't see clear,
Be still, my soul, to Him so dear,

He knows the way I stumbling take
And what my soul will holy make.
Though set about with many foes,
Be still, my soul, He knows, He knows.

November 2017

Be Merciful to Me

I am so ashamed, my Jesus,
Of my sins both great and small.
This my only consolation:
It is sinners that You call.
Those that think that they are righteous
In the things they do and say,
Missing by degrees perfection,
Cannot find the Narrow Way.
He who beats upon his bosom
And will not lift up his eyes
Pleading just Your blood and mercy,
He shall see the peaceful skies.

November 2017

Christmas Meditation

See where He in a manger lies
Whose glory fills the earth and skies,
Seed of the woman, born to die
That fallen men may live thereby.

What caused Him to descend so low
That He our mortal ills might know?
'Twas Mercy free, His crown above,
And it was coupled fast with Love.

He came to earth His bride to seek
And make her righteous, holy, meek.
The cost He paid, His very life
That He might have her for His wife.

Well might the skies with glory shine
While angels hymned the birth divine.
Blest grace that overcomes our Fall
And saves His own, both great and small.

December 2017

Communion Meditation

Blessed be our gracious God,
The unfathomed great I AM,
Blessed be His bread and wine:
They bespeak a roasted Lamb,
He that righteous wrath endured,
Though 'twas I that should have died,
Paschal sacrifice and meal,
Jesus Christ the Crucified.

December 2017

Denial and Restoration

(after the Rev. James McCarthy)

"I never will deny You."
I heard my proud heart say.
But in a few short minutes
My courage fled away.

For fear of just a servant
Your great Name I denied.
The rooster crowed, You looked at me
And my proud heart did chide.

I thought about Your warning,
How it I set aside.
It made me weep for sadness
That I had You denied.

Between me and the traitor
One difference I see
For You, my gracious Savior
Had made request for me.

You graciously restored me,
Removed my sin and shame
But not for my own merit
But that You love Your name.

Blest grace that did not leave me
To wallow in my sin,
Restored me to Your favor,
Commissioned me again.

December 2017

The Day After Christmas

'Twas the day after Christmas and all through the stores
There were customer service lines clean out the doors
Full of people returning the stuff that they got
From the horrible sweater to wi-fi crock pot.
For the trinkets and trifles of earth don't endure.
We have never enough, so we want more and more.
Man's heart has a vacuum of size most immense
That cannot be filled with the objects of sense.
There is only one vision that man satisfies:

'Tis the sight of his Maker, the Ultimate Prize.
Let me look past the presents and tinsel and tree
To the heavenly things that are waiting for me.

December 2017

Guilt and Pardon

'Twas I that led the rabble
That on You laid their hands
'Twas I that mocked and scourged You
Who heaven and earth commands.
'Twas I that held the hammer
That nailed You to the tree
For You were there for evil
That had been done by me.

If friend You did forgive me
'Twere more than I could see:
Instead You gave Your lifeblood
For me, Your enemy.
Blest mercy beyond measure
That cannot fathomed be
That drove my Lord to suffer
To win the likes of me.

January 2018

The Valley of Dry Bones

(After Mr. Stephen Spinnenweber)

I lay among the skeletons.
my bones were dry indeed.
How could I live that long lay dead?
What summons could I heed?

But then the Mighty Voice was heard
That first called light to be,
And reassembled were the joints
As anyone could see.

And flesh and sinews newly formed
Spread o'er me at command
And skin began to cover me,
Refashioned by His hand.

And then the mighty Spirit wind
Blew into nostrils still
And I awoke at His Command
In answer to His Will.

I did not raise myself nor could
I ready myself for
The grace He poured into my heart,
Full measure, running o'er.

Blest Grace that resurrects the dead,
That bids them live again
That they might Glorify His Name
Who gives His grace to men.

January 2018

False Witness

(After the Rev. James McCarthy)

Against You did they raise their voices,
Charging You with sin,
But could not even then agree
That they their case might win.

For no just cause they found to raise
Against the Righteous One.
The only sinless Man who lived,
Of God the only Son.

So strong their hatred of the Truth
That they might sin enjoy:
They'd rather murder Innocence
Than God's Name glorify.

But as for me, it is not hard
To find my every flaw:
One only needs to look into
The broken Ten-Word Law.

You were attacked by witness false,
Condemned instead of me
Who justly merits wrath untold:
How could this ever be?

Blest grace that took my burden's weight,
Let me instead go free.
Blest Savior, kind beyond all thought
That paid my debt for me.

January 2018

Ecclesiastes 3:16

Where Justice should have had her sway
There wickedness was found.
Where Righteousness was thought to be
Iniquities abound.

January 2018

Rescue

(After the Rev. Jim McCarthy)

In the dark, cold stall I lay:
Thought it might be my last day,
Sick, diseased, and broken sore
Lying on the stable floor.

Past prize-winning little lambs,
Past the burly, pleasant rams,
He drew near, beholding me
Dying in my agony.

"Give me that one," then He said.
"No, sir, that one's nearly dead."
"No, I'll have no lamb but she."
Thus He bought my liberty.

What the cost He had to pay?
From His own Son turned away,
Pouring out His anger strong
On the Son He loved so long.

Who can fathom Grace like His?
For no greater Love there is.
No analogy can trace
Height nor depth of Saving Grace.

January 2018

Shame (II)

(After the Rev. Jim McCarthy)

I it was, the guilty,
Without blemish You.
I deserved the mocking,
You were ever true.

I deserved the spitting
And the thorny crown.
You were ever holy,
By my guilt pressed down.

King they rightly called You,
Mockingly did bow,
You Who heaven worships
Ages long and now.

'Twas my shame You shouldered
That I might go free.
'Twas my sin You bore that
I might righteous be.

Blessed, sweet compassion,
O how can it be?
Mercy beyond measure
For the likes of me.

February 2018

Shame (III)

(After the Rev. Jim McCarthy)

With my curse You were crowned
The thorns were mine You wore.
The shame itself was mine
As was the cross You bore.

The darkened sky was mine,
Bereft of Blessed Face.
The guilt and wrath were mine,
Devoid of Saving Grace.

They took Your clothes away
Uncovering my shame.
They mocked and laughed and spat
Blaspheming Holy Name.

The Father could not bear
To look upon the Son
When laden with my guilt,
His Own Beloved One.

Propitiation made,
God's fury turned away,
He bade the sun to shine
Again upon that day.

All I deserved You bore
And gave me as my own
Your perfect righteousness
To wear before Your throne.

How could You spend Your life,
Your blood for such as I?
How could the Prince of Life
For such a sinner die?

Eternity is long,
But cannot well afford
Sufficient time to praise
The Mercy of my Lord.

February 2018

From Isaiah 66:2

Not to the self-important man
Nor he who thinks he's wise,
Not to the clever or the proud
Or good in his own eyes.
To this man will I look: he is
Regarded by his Lord,
Who has a humble, contrite heart
And trembles at My Word.

March 2018

From Hebrews 12:3

My soul, consider Him
Whom sinners did oppose,
Who contradiction faced
From His pernicious foes
Lest weary in the strife
Your heart should faint away,
Thus fail to overcome
This hot, contested day.
Your weapons keep at hand,
Your shield polish well
And fight with all your might
Against the hosts of Hell.
So, watch against yourself,
Against the world and sin.
With Heaven's grace bestowed
You shall the vict'ry win.

March 2018

From Philemon

(After the Rev. James McCarthy)

"Whatever he may owe, my friend,
Put that to my account.
I promise I myself will pay
To you the full amount."

So Paul became the Surety
For the useless runaway,
As Christ my debt did undertake
To free me on That Day.

For imputation laid my sins
Upon His spotless soul.
And all God's wrath, He satisfied,
Not partly, but the whole.

Blest Grace that paid what I could not
And kindly gave to me
His perfect righteousness so pure
That I His face may see.

March 2018

The Kingdom Grows

(After Mr. Stephen Spinnenweber)

The seed is planted in the earth.
Upon it shines the sun,
It grows apace to shoot and leaf
Though understood by none.

So Gospel seed may dormant lie
As years and years pass on
Then suddenly break through the earth
To greet the rising sun.

The Word of God cannot return
Unless His Will be done,
And He will grow the kingdom
That He promised to His Son.

With means or else without them,
In secret mystery:
Of His soul's pain, He promised Him,
That He would surely see.

March 2018

Storm

(After Charles Haddon Spurgeon)

> The billows still around me roll
> And crash against my feeble soul.
> Dark Providences I will bless
> Although they cause me great distress.
> The storm around me wildly rages
> But casts me on the Rock of Ages.

> *March 2018*

Genesis 22:8

> I had no offering to give:
> No perfect sheep, no spotless ram,
> But still I come to Heaven's King
> For God Himself provides the Lamb.

> No goodness to commend my soul,
> No righteousness in what I am
> But to the cross alone I cling:
> For God Himself provides the Lamb.

> The Son was disinherited
> And so the Father's child I am:
> He suffered for the guilt I bore,
> For God Himself provides the Lamb.

> *April 2018*

Psalm 23:5–6

> Though my enemies are near
> Yet Your table shall appear;
> An invited guest I am
> To the marriage of the Lamb.
> They who scoffed and mocked at me

Shall the final triumph see
Though they go to endless pain
I beside You will remain.
Justice shall be served at last
When this sorry world is past.
Blessed Life bestowed by Grace,
Ever to behold Your Face.

April 2018

To DHC

He Who knew your evil deeds
Though you lied to mortal men,
To His Throne shall summon you,
There to meet your guilt again.

There is just one Sacrifice
That can well for sin atone.
Seek forgiveness through His blood
Or else suffer Hell alone.

April 2018

Matthew 21:31

Lady Rahab shall go in
Likewise small Zacchæus too
To the Throne Room of the King,
Pharisee, ahead of you.

April 2018

Genesis 22:6 & John 19:17

As Isaac bore the wood
Up to the mountain high,
So Jesus bore the cross
On which He was to die.
God did not leave His friend
His only son to slay
But plunged Himself the knife
Of Justice on that Day
Into His only Son
That sinners He might save.
Blest mercy for this wretch
Who else had seen the grave.

May 2018

Communion Meditation (II)

How can the soul repine,
Desiring earthly things,
When feasting on the Grace
Of Christ, the King of kings?

May 2018

Matthew 9:2

Be of good cheer, my soul,
No matter what men say:
Christ, Priest and Sacrifice,
Has purged your sins away.

May 2018

I Corinthians 9:25

Take courage, O my soul,
And do not be afraid.
The crown you seek to gain
Cannot decay or fade.

Though you have little here
And may be quite obscure
The treasure that awaits
For you in Christ is sure.

May 2018

Sod Growing

(Psalm 104:14)

Outside my door I plainly see
A wonder way down low,
For He Who reigns in Heaven high
Still makes the grass to grow.

May 2018

On the Mental Illness of a Friend

My friend is sick and poor
But I with her must bear.
To bear infirmity
What Mercy must be there!
And so, my Lord, I see,
Though in a way so small,
How great your Grace to me
To bear my weakness all.

May 2018

A Secret Stranger

(After Jeremiah Burroughs)

> I am a secret stranger,
> Though I might live next door.
> To tarry here forever
> Is not what I seek for.
>
> I seek a better country,
> A city far more fair,
> With Jesus Christ, my Savior,
> And saints and angels there.
>
> That with propitiation
> I may behold His face,
> Corrected and perfected
> To feast upon His Grace.
>
> So if my earthly dwelling
> Be dark and poor and small
> I look off to the dwelling
> Where I shall "have it all."

June 2018

Damascus Road

> How great Your Grace to Saul must be:
> You blinded him that he might see.:

June 2018

Sweet Perfume: Exodus 30:37

No man may make a like perfume,
And he that does so meets his doom.
God will His honor safeguard thus
And bids His will observed by us.

June 2018

Invocation

Come, Sweet and Heav'nly Dove
Descending from on high:
Fulfill the Savior's love
In Mercy hov'ring nigh.

O come upon Your saint
With Unction and with Power,
To dead men giving Life,
Salvation in this hour.

June 2018

Trinity

You looked down from Your Throne
Upon the sons of men
Before the world was made,
Electing some of them
According to Your will,
O Father we adore
And bless You for Your love
Forever, ever more.

You came down from Your Throne
Into a cattle stall
Made like the sons of men
To save the wretched thrall.
And God the Father's will
You honored perfectly,
The only righteous Son,
Which we could never be.

You came down from Your Throne
In fiery tongues of flame
Salvation to apply
And honor Jesus' name.
You did not glorify
Yourself, but Christ the King,
For which, O Dove Divine,
To You we gladly sing.

Eternal Three in One,
Blest God Whom we adore,
Your church shall ever sing
Your praises evermore.
Eternal Three in One,
Eternal One in Three,
We bow before Your Throne
For all eternity.

July 2018

II Corinthians 4:8

The things that we can see
Shall pass away for sure
But those we cannot see
Forever will endure.

July 2018

For James Henley Thornwell

Though he be not extolled in song
The good man's shadow's always long.

July 2018

Praying for Grace

Though sins and weaknesses abound
And faults within reside,
Who prays for sanctifying Grace
Shall never be denied.

July 2018

From Isaiah 40–44

Sing, O my soul, to your Great King,
Though how you do not see
Since He has given you His Word,
Provision there shall be.

For He Who cleanses all your sin
For His Name's sake alone,
He shall provide your every need,
There shall not fail a one.

Who loved your father Abraham
And Jacob freely chose,
Providing for your deepest need,
He shall provide for those,

Your temp'ral needs
For clothes and meat,
For housing and for health,
So rest before His feet

And do not fear but wait for Him.
His praises you shall sing
And all His mercies hymn with joy
Who is your gracious King.

July 2018

Shortness of Breath

The Holy City shall be built
Though we cannot see how,
And we shall live in Heaven's joys
Who puff and struggle now.

July 2018

Exodus

We stand upon the Red Sea's shore:
No rescue is in sight,
And Pharaoh's host behind us stirs
All through the weary night.
But he who looks with eyes of flesh,
Forgetting might of God
Knows not the wave shall drown the foe
While we shall pass dryshod.

July 2018

Submission

The things Thou hast ordained,
Since they seem good to Thee,
Plant such grace in my heart
That they seem good to me.

July 2018

Be Still

Be dry, my tears and soft my cries,
Be done with murmured dust.
Who knows not that He will provide
Has not yet learned to trust.

July 2018

Philippians 4:6

Be still, my anxious soul,
And rather bow the knee.
Let your requests be known,
But do so thankfully.

July 2018

On Seeing a Full, Double Rainbow

(After Kathi Goodhart)

Hush, O my soul, in affliction.
See you do not complain.
You had not seen the rainbow
Had God not sent the rain.

August 2018

From Exodus 15

(After Rev. Josh Hinson)

But three days in the desert
We found ourselves athirst
We found but bitter water
For us to drink at first,

He Who the Red Sea parted
Did not from us depart
But tested us and proved us
For what was in our heart.

We murmured and we grumbled,
Forgetting Red Sea wave
Through which we passed unhindered
While Egypt found its grave.

But God in mercy tender
Made bitter water sweet
Providing what we needed,
What for our needs was meet.

Do not, my soul, in trouble
His Power great forget:
Canaan shall be your portion:
Your needs shall all be met.

August 2018

Looking to the Brazen Serpent

Though bitten by the serpent
And venom of my sin
In all my bloodstream coursing,
Iniquity within
Yet gazing on the serpent
By Moses lifted high,
To Him Who bore God's anger,
I know I shall not die.
Not at myself but Jesus,
His righteousness alone,
Though I am full of evil
He did for me atone.

August 2018

The Sharp Edge of Affliction

(After Mr. Stephen Spinnenwebber)

'Twixt the scalpel and the dagger
What the difference must be
Is the purpose of the person
Who is wielding one at me.
Though the edges of these objects
May be sharpened equally
In the hand of my Physician
Shall the scalpel healing be.
Though affliction cuts or pinches,
God knows what is best for me,
And the benefit eternal
Shall my soul forever see.

September 2018

Refuge (II)

(From Numbers 35)

Though I am guilty, gracious Lord,
I pray You let me hide,
And safely in the City
Of Refuge may abide.

Until the death of my High Priest
Who bears my sin away,
Restores me to my heritage
Upon the Judgment Day.

Bloodshed requires shedding blood
Else were the land defiled,
But Jesus' blood was shed for me
That I might be Your child.

So not for me but for His sake
I pray You wrath restrain.
His mercy, Lord, and Yours alone
Shall be my sweet refrain.

September 2018

Yom Kippur

So many beasts, so many years!
So much blood shed, So many tears
Until the Sacrifice alone
That could for human sin atone.
No more remembered year by year
For, reconciled, we no more fear.
No longer mourning, we rejoice
And praise the Lamb with cheerful voice.

September 2018

Theophany

(After the Rev. Dr. Donald McLeod)

The mountain with the fire blazed,
The people standing all amazed,
The trumpet sound, an awful blast,
The thunder and the lightning cast,
The Father came in cloud and fire
That He their reverence might inspire.
Obedience they promised there;
To hear His voice they did not dare.

The church within the upper room
Aware Christ rose from out the tomb
Awaits the Spirit from on high
Until He came that would draw nigh,
The mighty wind that on them blew
Though they were only but a few
And tongues of flame upon each brow
That they might herald Gospel now.

But in the darkened stable lies
Him born at last through virgin cries,
Not fire, but water and in blood
He came at last to make us good
And for His church He came to bear
The wrath that they would never dare.
With fire the Father, Spirit came
But not so with Emmanuel's name.

Though Justice ever sounds aloud
And Power can't be disallowed
Yet Grace comes softly, sweetly in
To souls all bound in chains of sin.
All gracious comings, but most sweet
The coming of His infant feet
To keep the law we broke for all
He lay within a cattle stall.

September 2018

On NOT Seeing a Rainbow

In difficulty struggling?
In sorrow or in pain?
One could not see the rainbow
Unless He sent the rain.
And though I do not see it,
Still praying for the sight,
Joy's coming in the morning
To chase the tearful night.

September 2018

From Psalms 13 and 28

How long will You forget me
And I in bitter pain
Cry out for grace and mercy,
Nor rescue see again?
O be not silent to me
Lest I be like the dead.
Provide for and protect me,
My Lord and living Head.
Let me not faint, deliver
And set my soul on high.
If You, Lord, do not answer
I fear that I shall die.

October 2018

Wallabies

The wallaby's a wanna-be
Or so at least it seems to me.
If he were really strong and true
No doubt he'd be a kangaroo.

October 2018

Emus and Effort

Though hard the emu bird may try
Without a doubt, he cannot fly.

October 2018

The Sacrifice of the Peace Offering

God's fiery anger burned You up
Yet still we feast on You.
We eat Your flesh and drink Your blood
And promise to be true.

As food gives strength for needed work
So as I feed on You
I feel life springing up again:
My God, my heart renew.

October 2018

(So far) Unanswered Prayer for Provision

Be still, my soul, when He hears not
Or to respond delays.
You cannot see a mighty work
In ordinary ways.

His work, oft hidden from your eyes,
Unfolding through the years,
Cannot be seen with naked eye
But only through your tears.

October 2018

From Psalm 27:14

Be brave, my fearful soul
And in His promise stand.
He can't deny Himself,
All things He does command.
He knows all of your needs,
He promised to provide.
In Providence then rest
And see your need supplied.

October 2018

From Psalm 40:17

Though I am small and powerless
As you can clearly see
Yet Heaven's King in mercy great
Is thinking about me.

October 2018

From Psalm 44:23–26

O You that never sleeps
I pray awake, arise.
You Who sees everything
From me hide not Your eyes.

You Who my prayer regards
I beg an answer still.
You Who controls all things
Grant me to know Your will.

You Who cannot be seen
Show Yourself now, I pray.
You, all longsuffering,
O hear my plea today.

October 2018

From I Samuel 18

(After Mr. Stephen Spinnenwebber)

As Jonathan loved David,
Their hearts together knit,
And clothed him in his garments,
That princes would befit
So did my blessed Savior
Despite my low estate
Bestow on me His raiment
Of righteousness so great,
Enough my sin to cover
My weakness and my shame.
He bore for me my burden
That I might praise His name.

October 2018

From Revelation 22

Amen! Come, gracious Lord
Who lives though You were dead.
Come Mighty Sovereign Prince,
Our Lord and living Head.

Conclude this sorry world,
All hist'ry being past,
The New Earth ent'ring in,
All evil gone at last.

Give us the water sweet
That from the Throne flows out.
Give us the tree of life
That all our ills shall rout.

Forever be our Light
That we in truth may see
The beauty of Your Face,
Your Mighty Majesty.

Forever shall we sing
Within the city wall
The praises of our King
Who overcame us all.

October 2018

From Psalm 37

O my soul, do not fret
Because of wicked men,
For they shall be cut down
And find at last their end.
Trust in the Lord, do good,
So you shall dwell in peace,
In famine shall be fed
And find your darkness cease.
Make Him your greatest joy
And He shall give to you
The other things you seek
Because His word is true.
Commit your way to Him
And wait His pleasure sure,
Acquitted shall you be,
For He shall find you pure.

Rest in the Lord and wait
'Til He shall please to act.
Turn not aside to sin:
He justice shall enact.
In just a little while
The wicked shall not be.
You'll search but find him not;
Instead the meek you'll see.
For earth to righteous men
For His sake shall belong.
They shall reside in peace
Through all the ages long.

Though bad men rise in hate
They can't you o'ercome
Because He fights for you
To bring you safely home.

Your heritage from God
Forever shall endure.
And you shall dwell in peace
Forever, ever more.
For meekness has reward,
The face of God to see;
His glory to behold
For all eternity.

November 2018

From Revelation 13:10

(For J. D. W. and J. I.)

You lead into captivity,
O men of evil might?
Do you not know the day shall come
When in my very sight,
From Holy wrath you'll shrink away
The tables turned about,
To your imprisonment that day
When Justice finds you out?

If with the sword the just you slay
With arrogance and pride
Do you not know when all is done
It shall be you that died?
This holds the faithful spirit up
in his perplexity.
Though Justice tarries, it shall come
But with finality.

November 2018

From Ezra 9:5

The evening sun was sinking low
When Ezra's pain did overflow:
The sin was great and full of shame,
Profaning God the Father's name,
But round the altar had been poured
Blood of the off'ring of the Lord.
His prayer he dared to lift on high
Because the offering was nigh.
He saw not only Justice pure
But mercy through which to endure.
Has made a way men may draw nigh.
And so we see not guilt alone
But Precious Blood that did atone.
Blest God, not leaving us in sin
But cleansing us, without, within.

November 2018

From Hebrews 6:19

Within the veil my Savior stands:
My name is written on His hands,
My only righteous Surety
Appears before my God for me.

November 2018

A Grasshopper

(From Isaiah 40:22)

I am a little insect,
A grasshopper by fame,
Of small repute and worthless
But yet I have a name.
Though weak and heavy laden
With trouble and distress,

He still sits in His heaven
My weary soul to bless.
Though I am weak and puny
His strength is still the same
And He will come to save me
For love of His own Name.

December 2018

Psalm 73

To Israel our God is good,
To those whose hearts are clean,
But I was nearly overcome
By what my eyes had seen.

The wicked prosper in this world,
A peaceful death they die,
They leave their substance to their babes
And others vilify.

But I am troubled every day
And chastened by and by.
So why did I my ways attend
And my heart purify?

For every day I am distressed
And stretched beyond my strength.
And every day I trouble find
Nor peace at any length.

If I speak thus I will offend
Against God's children all.
But in the temple did I see
What shall the proud befall.

For God shall cast them quickly down
To everlasting shame
And quite forgotten shall they be
When perishes their name.

My understanding, Lord, is small,
So brutish is my mind;
Before Your wisdom as a beast
Did You my spirit find.

On God then will my spirit wait
Until You rescue me,
For he who trusts in God alone
Shall peaceful future see.

January 2019

Still Waiting

When God deals with His children
Sometimes His help seems late.
The little ones He tends at once;
But older ones must wait.

A small child asks for trifles,
The older for supply.
I wait for His provision
And dare not ask Him why.

January 2019

From Psalm 107

O thank the Lord, for He is good:
His mercy lasts forever more.
Let those He has redeemed so state
To whom He gave His rescue sure.

He brought them back from East and West,
From North and South, from far beside,
Those who in deserts wandered lost
Nor city found where to abide.

Athirst and hungry, faint they cried
Unto the Lord most High above.
He led them safely through distress
Unto the city of His love.

O that all men would praise the Lord
For wonders to the sons of men.
He satisfies the longing soul
And makes the hungry full again.

Those once in chains of darkness bound
Afflicted and distressed, forlorn
Because they had His words despised
He suffered them in pain to mourn.

He brought them down with bitter toil:
They fell down and could not arise.
They cried to Him, He rescued them
And gave them light to cheer their eyes

O that all men would praise the Lord
For wonders to the sons of men.
He breaks the gates of brass apart
And shatters iron bars again.

Fools are afflicted for their sins
Their appetite flees far away
They draw near to the gates of death:
He rescues them as is His way.

O that all men would praise the Lord
For wonders to the sons of men.
Let them make sacrifice with joy
And offer Him their thanks again.

From I John 4

It wasn't that we loved You.
We hated You instead.
You could have just destroyed us
And left us all for dead.

But Grace in its perfection
Is found in You alone:
You sent Your Son to save us
And for our sins atone.

So when our brother stumbles
And heaps his sin above
If we know of Your mercy
We must respond in love.

His sins to cover over
As fully as we can
For he who loves the Father
Must love his fellow man.

February 2019

On Being Employed Once Again

(From Titus 2:8–10 and Ephesians 6:6–8)

Let me serve my earthly master,
Pleasing him in everything,
For with good will working for him
I am serving Christ my King.

February 2019

On Not Understanding my Steps

(From Hebrews 11:8)

> Though I know not where I'm going
> Let me to my oath be true
> For I cannot be mistaken
> While I follow after You.

March 2019

On Suffering

(From I Peter 3)

> Who will harm you, O my soul,
> If you walk in righteous ways?
> But if suff'ring is your lot
> And you toil through bitter days
> Think of Him Who went before:
> Innocent, He suffered harm
> All to bring His people home,
> And their cold affection warm.
> We like sheep had gone astray,
> Turning every one from good,
> But He offered up Himself
> For 'twas in our place He stood.

March 2019

On Suffering (II)

(From I Peter 4)

> To fortify yourself, my soul,
> Let this protect your mind:
> Our Blessed Lord bore pain for us
> So we shall surely find
> We face distress and bitter pain
> At times along our way.

It must be so until there comes
The great and final Day.
It is Christ's suff'rings that we share,
In body or in mind,
And sharing them, when He shall come,
We perfect joy shall find.
Though others may speak ill of us
And falsely us accuse
Still God is glorified in us,
Will not our souls refuse.
Do you not know He comes to judge
And perfect justice do?
You'll be acquitted on that day,
So there is hope for you.

March 2019

On Justice Delayed

(From Isaiah 40:27ff))

When Justice is denied
Or else at least delayed
Let this thought be your guide,
Let this truth be your aid:

The Everlasting God,
The Universal King,
Rules all things with His rod,
And all men low will bring.

He never sleeps or faints
Nor fathomed His thoughts be.
He shows unto His saints
His will by His decree.

Though Justice may be slow
It shall appear at last
And unrepentant foe
Into the fire be cast.

So patient shall you wait
Until the End shall come
Justice is never late,
And you shall rest at Home.

March 2019

"I Will Not Leave You Comfortless"

(From John 14:18)

Come, Sweet and Heav'nly Dove,
I need Your comfort now
For foes oppress my soul
Nor can I yet see how
This burden I can bear
For I am not a stone
Nor have I strength of rocks
To carry this alone.
How long will You stand by
And let my foes oppress?
And how long silent be
In view of my distress?
When will You comfort me
And cheer my heart so sad?
When will I blessing know
And find my spirit glad?

March 2019

Perseverance (II)

Though hanging here suspended
Between the earth and sky
And hearing all the mocking
Of many passers by,
With You my hard heart soft'ning
By mighty power divine
And giving me repentance

I call this Savior mine,
My heart will gather courage
If I should hear You say
That I will be beside You
In Paradise today.

April 2019

Perseverance (III)

(From Hebrews 12:8)

My soul, complain not when He smites
Or Providence adverse you see.
He whom the Father does not beat
A bastard son shall prove to be.

May 2019

On a Thunderstorm During Morning Worship

When from the darkened sky above
The mighty thunder peals
Or from Your dark and fearful wrath
The whole earth, shaking, reels,
Where can we find a place to hide
To keep us safe from You?
We run into the mighty Ark
Until the storm is through.
Because we could not face Your wrath
And since You loved us too
You gave us Christ in Whom we hide
And find our safety true.

May 2019

From Hebrews 12

Not to a desert mount
And tempest, storm, and gale,
Not to a trumpet's sound,
A louder, longer wail,

Not to a frightful peak
Aflame with lightning's blast,
Not to a dreadful Voice
At which they stood aghast,

Not to a quaking fear
That frightened Moses too,
Not to a burning Law,
But to the throne room true,

Unto God's Holy Mount,
The City of the Fair,
Jerusalem the Blest,
And many angels there,

To God the Judge of all,
And to the Church First Born,
To just men now complete,
To the eternal Morn,

To Christ Who stands between,
To Blood that speaks a word
Far better than the cry
Of Abel's blood earth heard.

We meet eternal things
That cannot pass away,
And Justice pure and high
That will be done some Day.

If they did not escape
Who from him turned aside
Let us with godly fear
Before Your face abide.

Therefore, bind up the knees
That feebly fail and fall.
Make straight paths for our feet
Lest we should perish all.

We cannot trifle here
Nor toy with Him in pride:
God's a consuming fire
In Whom we safe abide.

May 2019

The Mercy Seat

He sits upon a throne
Of Majesty and Fame,
Of Justice pure and high,
But Mercy is its name.

May 2019

The Best Lawyer

I have the world's best lawyer:
He doesn't charge a thing.
He represents my person
Before my God the King.

I need not fear the outcome
Though guilty I must be:
My advocate and Savior
Has paid the debt for me.

May 2019

On the Ordination of a Young Man

So evil seems the world,
So dark our hearts within,
What hope have we to fight
And real triumph win?

But He Who sits beside
The Majesty on High
Will build His church until
This world has passed us by.

The Conqueror above
Still give His gifts to men.
And He will surely triumph
Until the very end.

June 1, 2019

Chastisement (V)

I think I feel Your rod,
For chastening I deserve
My Holy, Gracious God,
For from Your ways I swerve.

I know that when You smite,
Tis not caprice or chance
But Father's discipline
To holiness enhance.

For unlike mortal men
Who may capricious be
The Father of my soul
Does what is best for me.

Let me my lesson learn
And all my ways amend,
Then shall I know I shall
Meet sweet and happy end.

June 8, 2019

The Friend of God

(From Isaiah 41:8)

Not only as His servant
Did God His blessing send
Unto the faithful's father:
He named him as His friend.

June 2019

Success

(After John Calvin)

My soul, O do not count success
the way the wicked do.
Ir is enough if you know God
and He is pleased with you.

June 2019

For Mrs. Emily Bever

Tell me, my dear, what do you see
Now that you've closed your eyes?
It is not sorrow, toil, nor pain
nor.grief nor sad surprise.

We see the things of sense and touch,
The temporal today:
You see the things invisible
that cannot pass away.

We see affliction's burden now
So heavy but so light.
You see the everlasting Day
And not the endless night.

We are cast down, but you have rest,
Your spirit now made pure,
And we shall see you yet again
When we shall reach that shore.

From Jordan did they take the stones
And piled them up high
That kids to come might see them there
And ask their fathers why.

So your long his'try in the Way
Stands pointing to the One
Who rescued you and brought you home,
Our Savior, God the Son.

July 2019

For D. and B. Holt

A father singing hymns,
A mother bowed in prayer,
What richer heritage
Have children anywhere?

They sang once in the choir
But now they sing above
Before their Savior's throne
In everlasting love.

July 2019

Victory

(After John Calvin)

> Courage, my soul, in your distress
> When He seems not to hear.
> He knows the pathway that you take
> And what will drive you near
> To value Him above all things
> And learn to wait His will.
> Though you be wounded in the fight
> The enemy can't kill.
> So wait and pray and pray and wait:
> The vict'ry is secure.
> He knows what is the best for you
> And what you can endure.

August 2019

Paul's Scars

(After Rev. Stephen Spinnenweber)
(From II Corinthians 11)

> The scars you carry, brother,
> The signs of pain and loss
> They are the true stigmata,
> The emblems of the cross.
>
> Refusing not to suffer
> For Christ the King of kings,
> And bearing for His honor
> So many evil things.
>
> He who for conscience suffers
> And will not turn aside
> Shall meet at last His Savior
> And find He was his guide.

August 2019

Giving

(II Corinthians 9:6–8)

'Tis God Who stirs the heart
To help our fellow saint
By giving to his need
Lest he, discouraged, faint.

And though, in mercy great
He gives the willingness,
He then pronounces it
A grace that He will bless.

God loves the man who gives
To ease another's plight,
Whose ministry of help
Becomes his Lord's delight.

But he who loaded down
With good things from above
And still forbears to help,
How in that man dwells Love?

September 2019

Giving (II)

(James 1:27)

What dare you think, my spirit,
That God to you will say
When you shall stand before Him
That Last and Dreadful Day?

Your sins are very many,
Your faults are not a few:
You have no claim to merit
But that He died for you.

Religion undefiled
And pure as it can be—
To visit widows, orphans
When need your eyes shall see.

Trusting only in His merit,
Dying, living, rising too,
You shall hear His commendation
Who has worked the grace in you.

September 2019

In the Wilderness

Give me grace to eat the manna
That you give me for my part
With a cheerful, sweet submission
And a happy, grateful heart.

September 2019

Following the Star

(After Rev. Stephen Spinnenweber)

You drove us far away
East from the garden's gate,
A Savior promised us
To save us e're too late.
And when the Dayspring came
We saw Your guiding star
And followed it at once,
Our journey from afar.
Back to the Presence sweet,
The Best of everything,
We bowed down at Your feet,
Our precious toddler King.

September 2019

Be Still, My Soul

(After John Calvin)

When dark temptation, fear, or pain
Is burdening my heart,
I must not rest on my own will
But yield to Him His part
To order things as He sees fit,
My portion to control.
Through sorrow I must persevere,
And He will make me whole
When I have learned to wait for Him
And humbly to obey,
And pray the painful circumstance
Will keep me in the Way.

September 2019

For a Young Pastor

(From I Timothy 4)

O let no man your youth despise
But rather an example be
In word, behavior, charity,
In spirit, faith, and purity.

Unto yourself take careful heed
and to your doctrine faithfully;
so shall you save yourself at last
And those that hear you eagerly.

Your precious gift see you upstir
bestowed by hands of presbyt'ry.
To reading give attention, and
in doctrine show no laxity.

Be nourished in the faithful Word,
and trust the saving God who lives.
For he shall have a real success
who to the truth attention gives.

A faithful Pastor, Christ's own gift,
you are, with many years to grow.
We'll seek to imitate your faith
And with you, then, to heaven go.

Praise God Who gives such gifts to men,
His holy church to edify:
Imperfect sinners, yet to truth
Will boldness do they testify.

Hope

(From Romans 5:2–5)

In all my tribulation
Which presses me so sore
I look to find the patience
With which I must endure.

For patience works experience
And from it hope comes round,
For troubles drive us swiftly
To Where our hope is found.

This hope can't be defeated
When Love is spread around.
Our Hope is in our Savior
In Whom our help is found.

October 2019

Self-Control

(From Proverbs 16:32)

> Give me grace to rule my spirit
> When adversity I see,
> And while waiting for Your rescue
> May I do so patiently.
>
> O come quickly to my rescue
> While I silent wait for You,
> And in humble, meek submission
> May I unto You be true.

November 2019

From John Calvin

(Malachi 3:17)

> You see my every weakness,
> Each fault and sin inside,
> Which makes me sometimes wonder
> If I will safe abide.
>
> But You have promised sweetly
> For Christ's sake to forgive,
> Let me despite my weakness
> With You forever live.
>
> Though all I do is tainted
> In mercy You will spare
> As fathers do their children
> That I may be Your heir.

November 2019

Blindness

(From John Calvin)
(Isaiah 42:16)

> I am blind, O gracious Savior,
> Condescend my soul to lead.
> I am weak, O hear my crying,
> Cheer my soul and meet my need.
>
> I don't understand my footsteps,
> I know not the proper way,
> Hardly bear what comes upon me,
> In affliction every day.
>
> Keep me from all self-reliance,
> Cast my soul upon Your grace,
> Then with safety shall I journey
> 'Til the time I see Your Face.
>
> For a blind soul is more blessed
> That for safety must be led
> Than the self-sufficient person
> Great, but only in his head.

November 2019

Matthew 5:7

(After Rev. Stephen Spinnenweber)

> Give me such a gentle spirit
> That when brethren injure me
> I may cast Your Love's sweet cov'ring
> Over their iniquity
> Lest if I should not forgive them
> I should prove bereft of Grace:
> Let me gently walk beside them
> Until we shall see Your face.

November 2019

I go A-Fishing

(After John Calvin)
(John 21:3)

> All night I toiled briskly
> But nothing did I catch.
> You did this so that glory
> From You I might not snatch
> Imagining provision
> Was by my hand obtained
> Instead of that Your mercy
> In Providence still reigned.
> O give me meek submission
> In want and plenty too
> That I in thanks for mercy
> May glory bring to You.

> *November 2019*

Christmas Thoughts

(After John Calvin)
(From I Timothy I1:1)

> Why came He to the manger
> For us to live and die?
> 'Twas God the Father sent Him
> His wrath to satisfy.
> 'Twas He that loved us sinners,
> In Justice made a way
> That He might justly pardon,
> For Christ did bear away
> Into the realm of darkness
> Our sins both great and small
> And gave to us His goodness
> To cover one and all.
> And God the Holy Spirit

To all His will apply
The pardon Jesus purchased
That we may live, not die.

December 2019

Condescension

When evil men show kindness
To those who are their own
It hints Your condescension
Who came down from Your throne,

The image of their Maker
Not utterly obscured
That we may in their kindness
Behold our blessed Lord

Who not for friends or fam'ly
Deigned to this world to come
That sinners trusting in Him
Be brought forever home.

December 2019

For J.E.

Rest now, dear friend, your travels o'er:
You safely passed cold Jordan's shore
And to the city entered in,
Your soul now cleansed from every sin,
Perfected, waiting till the Day
When heav'n and earth shall pass away.
You see your Savior face to Face
And rest at last in His embrace.
No more to doubt or fear or cry,
The former things are all passed by,
No pain, no sorrow, and no grief

To interrupt your sweet relief.
We mourn for you but soon shall see
Your face in God's own family—
Blest hope that spurs the Christian soul:
Christ won for us the vict'ry whole.

December 2019